Law Enforcement

Sheriffs and Deputy Sheriffs

by Michael Green

Consultant:
Lt. Larry Boss
San Mateo County Sheriff's Department
Redwood City, California

RiverFront Books

an imprint of Franklin Watts
A Division of Grolier Publishing
New York   London   Hong Kong   Sydney
Danbury, Connecticut

RiverFront Books
http://publishing.grolier.com

Library of Congress Cataloging-in-Publication Data
Green, Michael, 1952-
    Sheriffs and deputy sheriffs/by Michael Green.
    p. cm.—(Law enforcement)
    Includes bibliographical references and index.
    Summary: An introduction to the law enforcement officers known as
sheriffs and deputy sheriffs, including their history, functions, responsibilities,
equipment, and the criminals they target.
    ISBN 07368-0188-X
    1. Sheriffs—United States—Juvenile literature. [1. Sheriffs.
2. Occupations.] I. Title. II. Series: Green, Michael, 1952-
Law enforcement.
HV7979.G74 1999
363.28'2'0973—dc21

                                                        98-45157
                                                          CIP
                                                          AC

Editorial Credits
Connie Colwell, editor; Timothy Halldin, cover designer; Kimberly Danger
    and Sheri Gosewisch, photo researchers

Photo Credits
AM General, 40-41
Bette Garber, cover
Corbis, 8, 10, 13
Hans Halberstadt, 26
Impact Visuals/Jim West, 22
John S. Reid, 18
Los Angeles County Sheriff's Department, 36, 39
Mary E. Messenger, 6
Michael Green, 14, 21, 29, 31, 34, 47
Shaffer Photography/James L. Shaffer, 32
Uniphoto/Daemmrich, 4, 16, 25

Table of Contents

Chapter 1

Sheriffs and Deputy Sheriffs

Sheriffs and deputy sheriffs are law enforcement officials. Their job is to maintain order. The duties of sheriffs and deputy sheriffs vary from department to department. But most sheriffs and deputy sheriffs keep order in three ways. They help prevent crime. They keep county courts safe. They also run county jails.

Sheriffs

Most U.S. sheriffs are county sheriffs. States are divided into small sections called counties. There are more than 3,000 counties in the United States. Almost every U.S. county has a sheriff.

Sheriffs maintain order in U.S. counties.

Deputy sheriffs assist sheriffs in many ways.

People elect most U.S. sheriffs. Only
citizens in Rhode Island and Hawaii do not
elect their sheriffs. Government officials select
the sheriffs in these states. In Canada, the
government appoints sheriffs.

Deputy Sheriffs

Sheriffs appoint deputy sheriffs to help them
maintain order. Sheriffs can appoint more than

one deputy sheriff. Some sheriffs in large counties appoint thousands of deputy sheriffs.

Deputy sheriffs assist sheriffs in many ways. They help guard county courts. They help operate county jails. Some deputy sheriffs even patrol streets and county roads to enforce county laws.

Reserve Deputy Sheriffs

Reserve deputy sheriffs are volunteers. These deputy sheriffs work without pay. Most reserve deputy sheriffs are ordinary citizens who volunteer to help sheriffs departments.

Reserve deputy sheriffs are similar to deputy sheriffs. They receive the same training as deputy sheriffs. Reserve deputy sheriffs also wear the same uniforms as deputy sheriffs. They perform many of the same duties. They help prevent crime. They enforce laws. But the main duty of most reserve deputy sheriffs is to respond to emergency calls. These emergency duties can include finding lost hikers or rescuing people trapped on cliffs.

Chapter 2

History of Sheriffs

Sheriffs have been maintaining order for more than 1,000 years. Sheriffs first kept order in what is now England. People from this area brought their ideas about sheriffs to North America.

The First Sheriffs

The word sheriff comes from the Anglo-Saxon words shire and reeve. Around the year 700, the Anglo-Saxons lived in what is now England. Anglo-Saxon families lived together in shires. Shires were like today's counties. Each shire had a chief. This chief was called the Reeve. People later combined these two words to form the word sheriff.

English kings used sheriffs to collect taxes and deliver official papers.

Many of the first European settlers in North America came from England.

These early sheriffs were like today's police officers. They maintained order. They made sure citizens obeyed laws. But early sheriffs also were different than today's police officers. These early sheriffs followed the orders of the king of England. They collected taxes and delivered messages for their king.

First Sheriffs in North America

Many of the first European settlers in North America were from England. These settlers brought their ideas about shires with them to North America. The English settlers formed new shires. These settlements became known as counties.

The first counties in North America were formed in Virginia in 1634. The king of England still controlled most of the sheriffs in these counties. These sheriffs collected taxes for the king. They also enforced the king's laws in the North American counties. But they had extra duties. For example, these sheriffs handled prisoners and ran county jails.

In the 1700s, counties began electing their own sheriffs. These sheriffs no longer had to follow the orders of the king of England.

The American West

In the 1800s, some Americans started to move west. Most of these settlers were trappers and fur traders. In the 1840s, families began to move west to look for new land and jobs.

These people established towns and counties in the West. The settlers formed town governments. Members of these governments hired sheriffs to keep order in the new counties.

Sheriffs in the West sometimes needed help to keep order. Most sheriffs hired deputy sheriffs to assist them. Deputy sheriffs helped the sheriffs make arrests and handle prisoners.

Western Sheriffs

Some sheriffs in the West were not honest. For example, the sheriff of Ada County, Idaho, stole horses from the citizens. This made the citizens of Ada County angry. They hung the sheriff. Other citizens in the West put dishonest sheriffs in jail.

Some sheriffs and deputy sheriffs became famous gunfighters. Bat Masterson was one such sheriff. Masterson was deputy sheriff of Dodge City, Kansas, in 1876. He fought many gun battles.

Bat Masterson was a famous sheriff and gunfighter in the late 1800s.

Chapter 3

Sheriffs Departments

No two sheriffs departments are exactly alike. But there are two main types of sheriffs departments. These are full-service departments and limited-service departments. These types of sheriffs departments have some things in common. They each prevent crime, protect county courts, and run county jails. But they also have some differences.

Full-Service Departments

Full-service departments are large enough to provide patrol services for their counties. These departments have enough deputy sheriffs to help police departments with patrol duties. For

Full-service departments are large enough to provide patrol services for their counties.

Sheriffs and deputy sheriffs in full-service sheriffs departments enforce traffic laws.

example, the San Mateo County Sheriff's Department has 500 employees. Almost 300 of these are deputy sheriffs.

Deputy sheriffs at full-service sheriffs departments perform the same duties as other deputy sheriffs. But deputy sheriffs at full-service departments help with patrol duties.

Limited-Service Departments

Limited-service departments are the other type of sheriffs departments in the United States. They are called limited-service departments because their deputy sheriffs do not have patrol duties.

Most limited-service departments are small. Many have fewer than 50 deputy sheriffs. Limited-service sheriffs departments do not have enough deputy sheriffs to help patrol their counties. Members of police departments patrol these areas instead.

Headquarters

All sheriffs departments have an important building called headquarters. County sheriffs work at their headquarters. Sheriffs give orders to deputy sheriffs from headquarters.

Headquarters is the most important building of a sheriffs department. Headquarters usually is the largest building of a sheriffs department. It sometimes is the only building for some small sheriffs departments.

Divisions and Bureaus

Large sheriffs departments are divided into divisions. Divisions are like small sheriffs departments. For example, each division has its own headquarters. Each division also has its own commander or captain.

Members of each division have different duties. Some members are patrol deputies. Others are detectives or correctional officers. Correctional officers handle prisoners. Some division members are office workers.

Divisions are divided into bureaus. Members within a bureau all perform similar tasks. For example, members of a detective bureau work together to solve certain types of crimes. Members of an emergency services bureau work together to help with emergencies. They may search for people who get lost. They may rescue people who are trapped on cliffs.

Sheriffs Department Positions

Members of sheriffs departments have different amounts of authority. Each sheriffs department

Headquarters is usually the largest building in the sheriffs department.

has one sheriff. The sheriff has the most authority in the sheriffs department. The sheriff is in charge of all other department members.

The sheriff in a large sheriffs department sometimes has authority over many department members. For example, the sheriff has authority over the undersheriff. The sheriff appoints this official to help with the sheriff's duties. The sheriff sometimes commands other department members called assistant sheriffs, chiefs, and commanders. Some sheriffs also command captains, lieutenants, and sergeants.

Sheriffs also have authority over deputy sheriffs. There are more deputy sheriffs in sheriffs departments than other kinds of officers. There are about 150,000 deputy sheriffs in the United States today.

Members of sheriffs departments have different amounts of authority.

Chapter 4

Training

Most sheriffs and deputy sheriffs have special training. This training helps sheriffs and deputy sheriffs learn the best ways to maintain order in their counties.

Sheriffs Training

Many sheriffs are highly qualified officials. Most sheriffs have college educations. Some have advanced educations in criminal justice, law, or public management. Many sheriffs start as deputy sheriffs. These deputy sheriffs can be elected as sheriffs after years of experience and training.

Many sheriffs complete training programs in law enforcement. For example, they may attend the Federal Law Enforcement Training

Many sheriffs have college educations.

Center (FLETC) in Glynco, Georgia. These training programs help sheriffs learn the best ways to maintain order and enforce laws in their counties. These programs also help sheriffs learn to use their weapons safely.

Many sheriffs continue learning about law enforcement after they finish their training programs. Sheriffs may take extra courses at the training schools. They also may attend meetings on law enforcement.

Deputy Sheriffs Training

People who want to be deputy sheriffs must apply for the position. Applicants must be at least 18 years old. Applicants must be 21 years old for some sheriffs departments. Applicants must have high school educations. They must have drivers' licenses. They also must be in excellent health and be physically fit.

Sheriffs department officials choose qualified applicants. The applicants then take a written test. The officials interview them. The applicants also take a medical test to make sure they are in good health. People who pass all these tests can become deputy sheriffs.

Sheriffs and deputy sheriffs have training programs to help them learn how to use their weapons.

Some applicants serve as other law enforcement officials but want to become deputy sheriffs. For example, a correctional officer may want to become a deputy sheriff. Some of these officials have attended FLETC or completed other training. These people usually do not need to take the written tests to become deputy sheriffs.

Chapter 5

Special Operations

Sheriffs department duties sometimes can be very dangerous. Sheriffs departments have special groups of deputy and reserve sheriffs to perform certain dangerous tasks.

SWAT Teams

Many sheriffs departments have Special Weapons and Tactics (SWAT) teams to perform dangerous tasks. Members of these SWAT teams are specially trained deputy sheriffs. These deputy sheriffs train to use special weapons to control especially dangerous situations. Riots are one type of dangerous situation. Large groups of people act violently during riots. Riots are

Specially trained deputy sheriffs serve on SWAT teams.

difficult to control. Members of SWAT teams are specially trained to control riots.

Members of SWAT teams wear special uniforms. Most SWAT team uniforms are black. Black uniforms are difficult to see at night. This makes it easier for SWAT teams to surprise suspects. Other SWAT team uniforms are designed for camouflage. Camouflage helps SWAT teams blend in with their surroundings. Members of SWAT teams also wear armored vests under their uniforms. These vests protect members from gunfire.

Members of SWAT teams use special weapons and vehicles. These weapons include pistols, shotguns, machine guns, and rifles. Members of SWAT teams only use their weapons when necessary. Some SWAT teams have armored vehicles. These vehicles protect SWAT teams from gunfire while they are traveling to crime scenes or riots.

Bomb Squads

Sheriffs departments sometimes need to disarm bombs. Some sheriffs departments have bomb

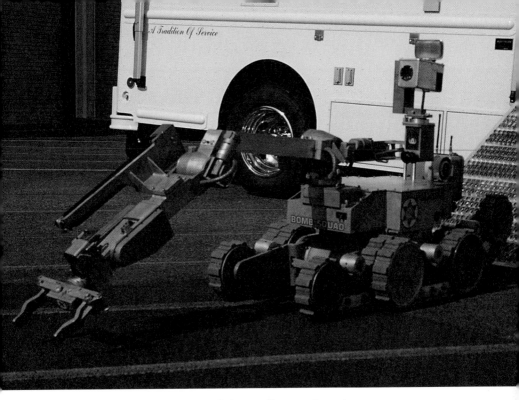

Bomb robots help technicians disarm bombs.

squads to take apart bombs and make them harmless. Bomb squad members have special tools and training to take apart bombs. These members are called bomb technicians.

Bomb technicians sometimes use bomb robots to help them disarm bombs. The technicians operate the robots by remote control. The robots have cameras attached to them. The cameras show the bomb technicians what the robots are doing. Bomb technicians operate the robots to take apart the bombs.

Sometimes bomb technicians cannot use robots to disarm bombs. Then bomb technicians need to disarm bombs by themselves. Bomb technicians wear armored bomb suits for protection when they disarm bombs.

Rescue Units

Sheriffs departments sometimes help with natural disasters or other emergencies. Many sheriffs departments have rescue units to help with these situations. These rescue units have different names at different sheriffs departments. Some are called Emergency Operations Bureaus (EOB) or Emergency Services Bureaus (ESB).

These bureaus have groups of people with special skills. Each group has different skills. Some groups know how to help people trapped or lost in mountains. Other groups know how

Rescue units help sheriffs departments with dangerous rescue missions.

to rescue people underwater. Each group knows how to handle different emergencies.

Many rescue unit members are volunteer reserve deputies. Full-time deputies are in charge of these officers on rescue missions. Some sheriffs departments have hundreds of volunteers in their rescue units.

Chapter 6

Patrol Vehicles

Full-service sheriffs departments use different vehicles to perform patrol duties. These vehicles include cars, off-road vehicles, motorcycles, and bicycles. Some sheriffs departments also patrol with boats, airplanes, and helicopters.

Cars

Most sheriffs departments patrol with cars. Deputy sheriffs can quickly patrol large areas in cars.

Sheriffs departments use cars that are similar to regular cars. But sheriffs departments' cars have special equipment to help them patrol. These cars have two-way radios. These radios allow deputy sheriffs to listen to messages from

Most members of sheriffs departments patrol with cars.

Some sheriffs departments use off-road vehicles to patrol unpaved roads.

headquarters. They also allow deputy sheriffs to send messages back to headquarters.

Most sheriffs departments' cars have lightbars. A lightbar is a set of plastic lights attached to the top of the car. The lights flash red and blue when the driver turns them on. Deputy sheriffs use this lightbar to show people there is an emergency. The lightbar warns motorists to move out of the way.

Sheriffs departments' cars also have sirens. A siren makes a loud noise when the driver turns it on. The loud siren sound tells people that a sheriffs department's car is nearby. The sound warns people to move out of the way.

Off-Road Vehicles

Some counties have unpaved roads. It is difficult to drive cars on roads that are not paved. Sheriffs departments then use off-road vehicles to patrol these areas.

Off-road vehicles can drive over all types of land. Many of these vehicles have four-wheel drive. Power from the engine turns all four wheels of a four-wheel-drive vehicle. This helps keep these vehicles from getting stuck in mud or snow.

Sheriffs departments' four-wheel-drive vehicles have radios, lightbars, and sirens. They also have winches to help them pull stuck vehicles out of ditches.

Some sheriffs departments use All-Terrain Vehicles (ATVs) to patrol. ATVs are small four-wheel-drive vehicles. Only one person

Sheriffs departments use boats to patrol on water.

can ride on an ATV. Sheriffs departments often use ATVs to patrol beaches.

Motorcycles and Bicycles

Some sheriffs departments use bicycles or motorcycles to patrol. These patrol vehicles are smaller than cars or off-road vehicles. Deputy sheriffs on motorcycles or bicycles can patrol crowded areas. Deputy sheriffs on bicycles also can patrol sidewalks and parks. Sheriffs and deputy sheriffs in cars cannot patrol these areas.

But motorcycle and bicycle patrols have some problems. These vehicles only have two wheels. This makes it easier for them to tip over on wet or slippery roads. Motorcycles and bicycles also do not have roofs. This makes these vehicles difficult to use in bad weather. Most modern sheriffs departments only use bicycles and motorcycles for special jobs.

Boats

Sheriffs departments sometimes need to patrol rivers, lakes, and beachfronts. Sheriffs departments use boats to patrol these areas.

Most sheriffs departments use standard speedboats with extra equipment. This equipment includes radios, lightbars, and sirens. Some boats have spotlights to help deputy sheriffs see at night. Some also have radar machines. Radar stands for Radio

Detecting and Ranging. Radar machines send out radio beams. These beams bounce off solid objects and come back to the radar machines. Deputy sheriffs can identify solid objects with radar machines.

Airplanes and Helicopters

In 1929, the Los Angeles County Sheriff's Department (LACSD) formed an aviation unit. This department used airplanes to move prisoners to jails. The aviation unit also helped find people lost in mountains. But airplanes sometimes are difficult to use. Airplanes need large spaces to land and take off.

In the 1960s, the LACSD and other sheriffs departments started using helicopters to patrol. Helicopters can land or take off in small spaces. Helicopters can patrol a few hundred feet above the ground. Members of sheriffs departments can see large areas from helicopters. Helicopters have powerful searchlights for night patrol.

Some large sheriffs departments have helicopters to help them patrol.

Maintaining Order

Sheriffs and deputy sheriffs work together to protect the lives of all the citizens in their counties. They help prevent crime, protect county courts, and run jails.

Sheriffs departments help maintain order across the United States and in parts of Canada. Sheriffs and deputy sheriffs are an important part of law enforcement.

Sheriffs Department Off-Road Vehicle

Winch

Tires

Lightbar

Sheriffs Department Labels

First Aid and Rescue Equipment

Words to Know

bomb technician (BOM tek-NISH-uhn)—someone who is trained to disarm bombs

bureau (BYUR-oh)—part of a sheriffs department that provides a certain service

camouflage (KAM-uh-flahzh)—coloring or covering that makes people blend in with their surroundings

county (KOUN-tee)—a part of a state with its own local government

disarm (diss-ARM)—to take a bomb apart so it cannot explode

elect (i-LEKT)—to choose someone by voting; people elect most sheriffs in the United States.

headquarters (HED-kwor-turz)—the place from which an organization is run; every sheriffs department has a headquarters.

maintain (mayn-TAYN)—to continue something and not let it come to an end; sheriffs and deputy sheriffs maintain order.

radar (RAY-dar)—a machine that can find solid objects by sending out radio beams; radar stands for Radio Detecting and Ranging.

riot (RYE-uht)—a group of people acting noisy, violent, and out of control

volunteer (vol-uhn-TIHR)—a person who offers to do a job, usually without pay

winch (WINCH)—a machine made of cable wound around a crank that helps lift or pull heavy objects; sheriffs departments use winches to help pull stuck vehicles out of ditches.

To Learn More

Green, Michael. *Bicycle Patrol Officers.* Law Enforcement. Mankato, Minn.: RiverFront Books, 1999.

Green, Michael. *Bomb Detection Squads.* Law Enforcement. Mankato, Minn.: RiverFront Books, 1998.

Green, Michael. *Motorcycle Police.* Law Enforcement. Mankato, Minn.: RiverFront Books, 1999.

Green, Michael. *SWAT Teams.* Law Enforcement. Mankato, Minn.: RiverFront Books, 1998.

Useful Addresses

Los Angeles County Sheriff's Department
Sheriff's Headquarters Bureau
4700 Ramona Boulevard
Monterey Park, CA 91754-2169

National Sheriffs' Association
1450 Duke Street
Alexandria, VA 22314-3490

San Mateo County Sheriff's Office
400 County Center
Redwood City, CA 94063-1655

Internet Sites

Hudson County Sheriff's Office
http://www.sheriff.bayonne.net

Los Angeles County Sheriff's Department
http://la-sheriff.org

National Sheriffs' Association
http://www.sheriffs.org

San Mateo County Sheriff's Office
http://www.smcsheriff.com

Index